WAY OF TIME

Leslie McMillan

Presentation by *BookLeaf Publishing*

Web: www.bookleafpub.com

E-mail: info@bookleafpub.com

ISBN: 9789360940249

First edition 2024

*For the love of my family, forever and
always, nana.*

PREFACE

One's journey path is honored by waking with gratitude, reflecting on life lived and having abundant hope for tomorrow. Time spent following you passion puts you on the right path.

GREY EYE'S BAR, SOUTH MOUNDS

I addressed him as Mr. Watkins
when working at my granddad's hardware store.
I sold him hog wire and six penny nails.
In Grey Eyes, he was Smitty.

We Bobcat cheerleaders
slipped away on hot Saturday nights.
Our folks thought we were taking in a film
across the river. They'd be shocked
if they knew we were shooting down beer
with black kids in the colored part of town.

Smitty had a "Yo da boss" attitude and a daughter
named Liz. She taught me to dance in that shack.
Smitty was a hoochy-coochy man,
his guitar whined like a woman coming.

And I don't know
if I was dizzy from the Mad Dog, or the blues
but I always ended up light headed, drunk
from his hand on my cheek.

Around 71 we started losing touch,
we seemed to scatter like jacks on concrete.
I left the Mississippi for the Rockies
after I got my degree, heard Kathy Malley

now lives in Tennessee. Liz got pregnant
by one of the Kerby boys, moved to Detroit
and had a son.

Smitty shut down Grey Eyes when glaucoma
took his sight, then he passed
away. We all showed up
for the funeral, drove down that gravel road,
shot down some beer
and watched the shack turn grey.

THE POINT

It was a meeting place. After church
our folks packed hot dogs
and headed for the picnic tables.
Bare chested dads played
pitch and catch, and moms wore shorts.

We kids fished for catfish
with bread balls on our hooks,
or explored the restroom-lookout
shaped like a ship.

Tourists with cameras clicked snap shots
where the Mississippi and Ohio met,
merged downstream, formed a giant Y.
They'd visit Magnolia Manor on a
brick road. A mansion on Park
where Grant slept. Paid a buck
to see the bed.

Even later, in Joy's Chevy we'd drive
the Cairo strip. Hit the Pit
for coke and fries. Watched Bagby
in his red GTO, cruise Commercial
looking for an easy
to take to the levee.

Joy and I'd meet the gang
at the Point and shoot bottle rockets

off the bank from long neck Bush bottles.
Drank Boone's Farm "Mellow Days" and
"Easy Nights". We'd stay
way past dark.

Bagby showed up and combed his hair,
leaning on his hood, begging for a beer,
or a girl to come steer his goat to the levee.
Our thoughts weren't muddy like the Mississippi,
they were clear like the Ohio.

Bagby could go jump
in either river, for all we cared.

ATONEMENT

I had to take them both.
I remember once saying to my mother
I want to have two
and she said, you can't
have both puppies, dolls.

Now driving too fast, passing two semi's on my right,
committed in darkness that rose and fell
through my stomach. Blending night sky and asphalt
with the roaring eyes of God
approaching, flashes of my mother
in Charlie's grocery store.
She stood by the potato bin.
Commanding me to open my hand,
where 2 tiny potatoes hid.
Red marbles for my pocket.

God looks for me.
Put them down, she said,
go tell Charlie now.
The she picked up the tiny potatoes
still warm from my skin and pushed the potatoes
back in my palm, and I worried for them.

Still round and whole I hoped.
Like Charlie's eyes. His white butcher apron
stained from beef,
standing like Mother Mary would stand

if she were Charlie.

And he touched my head, smoothing my hair
static electricity was everywhere
when Charlie cupped my hands
and said,
take them both.

MOUND CITY CALLS

Don't get in Mrs. Wingo's garden,
mama, she's insane. Instead
we'll sneak in her yard at night
and pick cataphyll. Smoke it
early summer behind the shed
in the cornfield. Late summer,
the pods are stuffed with worms,
we'll ride our bikes
to Cache Creek, catch gar
and dunk our heads.

Mama, I'll race you up Cemetery Hill,
we'll spend the night, run away,
put cheese salad sandwiches in a sack,
look for that homemade headstone
with marbles stuck in it.
Pretend to be Marilyn Monroe.

Come with me to the levee, mama,
we'll put our initials in a fence post,
put locust shells in our pockets,
make necklaces of clover.

Mama, I know it's impossible.
But, I'll quit my job, mama,
be home next week.
Rob a bank. Kidnap you
from the hospital. Take the tubes
from your nose and tie up the nurse.

I'll steal my bosses black Seville,
we'll go for a ride on the trail Of Tears,
eat hot dogs. Search the sloughs for tadpoles
scoop them in our hats.
Make pots with gumbo, bake them
in the sun. Cook mud stew.
Drop our clover leis in the river
and watch the undertow take them
down. Make a wish. Scrape the mud
from our feet, it's getting dark.
Put on your shit kickers, mama,
let's shake the dust.

RESONANT RAIN

The windows of my house were left open
when it rained. I could smell the Illinois Central.
See tracks laid out, north to south through
cloudbursts,
and casements pushed by rough hands. I was too
small then
to reach the sash and pull it shut.

My windows faced the shadowy side
of my house, where oak tree roots protruded
into the groundwork, branches struck the siding.
I think it must have rained often in my room
and washed the color from my walls.

It was like standing on the tracks waiting
for the roar. A resonance of steel to rain,
rain to steel, a rumble on my roof, the beat
of soppy ties under wheels. Watching trains
pump past hills on their way to Chicago
or New Orleans.

The brown boxcars
exceeded my ability to focus, their speed,
my head shaking no, into a blur
at that age. I couldn't count the cars anymore
than I could count the drops of water
hitting my floor.

A resound of it's passing shook my room,
shattered glass from my window frames,
and lifted me off the jagged ground
held warm by a sound
vibrating down from the depths of heaven.
Oblivious to the on-going downpour.

LONG WINTER, WARM BARN

It was January in Massac County
when Dan called me to the barn
and said, Look at all this alfalfa,
this old dirt
we still drag life out of.

Then he exhaled white puffs of air
and put two fingers to his lips
and said, Do you remember pretending
to smoke like this as a kid?

Said, remember building straw forts?

Said, Remember riding bikes up Cemetery Hill
at midnight and jumping off fences?

I drew in winter air like a school girl,
sent it to the roof and blew crystal kisses
toward his face and said, I remember
Buster, my rabbit. My dog Basil and a field mouse
I bought for a quarter.

Said, I remember chiggers, hair ribbons
and mud pies.

said, I remember rolling in the grass

and your wet kisses.

said, You old farmer, come here
as I unbuttoned his shirt,

said, nothing.

LEGACY FIELD

I never knew her name
but her house stood here once.
You can see the foundation
if you kick the ground.
She'd planted bulbs
all around this house
on her knees.
When I plowed in the spring
bricks came up and old milk bottles,
then midsummer, the beans. Sparse,
showing where I'd hit the hydraulic
up and over.
Being too hard on my on my John Deere
and me, I quit tearing up her yard.
Let it sit.

It's the place I walk to now,
when my cows won't come
when I call them: mmmbosssseee, aabossseee
Grain in a bucket.
They're not hungry, they're lazy.
And I know what I am.
So I walk the fence-row
up the ridge to her house
where daffodils still come up
in squares.

WALNUT TREES

Dan with his bolts in the barn
clanking around, off to bush-hog
the hill we've secretly been planting,
over the years. I say it's too steep
to disc, crack a hip
like Biffel did last year
when his John Deere reared.
Who wants beans there anyhow?

Look at him Jupe. he don't listen,
and out saplings will snap,
while he curses the lay of the land.
Today we'll go there, to our spot
and watch him.

Dan's great grandfather ran pigs
down that holler and his grandmother
fed gypsies that camped over there.
Even his dad tried to clear it once.
He gave up. I think it was meant
to be a woods.

I have to lift you over the ditch
and walk slowly now. Remember the walnuts
thrashing through these trees
and you retrieving them, but not all.

Now we can rest on the ridge,

me with my back against the poplar
and you biting at a cocklebur.
As I dig in your fur, picking them out

I look toward the dust
wailing up out of the ground
from our infant woods. I take a walnut
lodged under my butt, pitch it.
Grab another, heave it
in Dan's direction. I say, easy Jupe,
patting your old ready haunches,
these are for me.

SAVE THE HAY

We walk fast on Lovers' Lane,
the tractor's down, the truck
in use. A dirt road flanked
with woods, toting sandwiches
and cool water, looking
for the baler.

Where sweaty boys buck bales
into a flatbed truck, three cents
a bale, and Dan in the back
stacks the gold bars.
Itchy and hungry by now,
spitting alfalfa
from his mouth.

This morning over eggs,
I swatted flies. The radio said
sky's clear.
Man those boys can eat.
Two dozen eggs I fried,
then I sopped the leftover yolks
in toast crust and fed it to you.

The holes in my sweatshirt sleeve,
evidence of your teeth tugging me
to come see the gopher you shook
to death. Now prancing
like a horse at the county fair,

my proud collie. No sticks today,
I'm sorry.

No fence row play.
It's time now to rush and find
our men, before the rain comes
and combusts our gold into flame.
I can smell the clouds.

AFTER SHOCK

Sometimes life breaks our back
at the waist. Those that surround us
shake their heads,
throw up their hands
in attempts to release blame.
We are told to lie flat
for months. Lie flat and still.

I took her in
my skinny friend with pecan eyes
and fed her and her four children
spaghetti, fed her more pasta
than I could afford.

Late at night we'd stay up
talking about men's muscles
like seventh graders.
Scrapping sauce from plates,
I place my secrets on her fork.

Our stories came up like bubbles
from the salted water I put on the stove.
Hers, of doing married men, taking home
drunk cowboys from Dickies club, of stealing
best friend's lovers.
She rocked pride in her hand
lifting it like her Bud.

My stories had the bite of oregano,
seasoned and strong,
of my failed marriage,
the old bruises about my neck.
I told her of Rod, my rocket
I'd fallen for, like noodles
bent and conforming to the pot,
lying there waiting to soften,
to be eaten.

How could she have
not known, when she slept with him
that Wednesday in his maroon sheets,
night after night,
when sitting at my kitchen table
she'd tasted my heart.

SOUL ON FIRE

What has happened to my life?
I woke this morning and fire
had charred my walls. My room
gutted, nothing left inside.

And my husband is missing.
While I slept an inferno
burnt down our home. Sixteen years
and he leaves me now, to go
drink with his lover.

He sleeps with her on the seat
of his truck, meets her at the gym.
Acts cocky, like I don't know.
In anger, I call him a fucker,
something I thought I'd never do.

He looks around at the blackened frame
and says, "It must have been hot today."
I scream. He lies.
He yells. I cry.

But at night, after he's had enough of her,
he passes out in bed. I lay by him.
I close my eyes and pretend.
I pretend everything's alright.

Pretending helps me sleep at night.

When I wake he's gone to her.
I walk through rubble. Stir sad coffee.
Hope falls
like the skin from my bones.
I think I've died in the blaze.

THE SMELL OF BEER

He's drinking again. Out back
in a lawn chair, thinking as he does
with a six pack of Bud. Sitting on a slab
of concrete he'd poured back in nineteen
fifty five. Foot prints date it.
Imprints of a three year old, filled
with silt, her name wearing away.
Sometimes he'd sit and dig
at the dirt, brush it off, then trace
the lines. Up. Down.

This house built on stilts, the color of loam, river
stained
from the flood of '37, raised
by cinder blocks high enough
to hit geese gliding in perfect
formation, or drive a truck under,
even today is the same.
She'd go underneath to hide,
but first she'd count
the joists one at a time, checking
for spiders and wasps.

Seventeen steps to the front porch
then the door, the hardware floor,
where years before she'd placed a suitcase.
He never tried to stop her, turned his back
walked outside. Now she's returned

like a goose on a migrational stop.
She still hates his stale whiskey odor,
it strikes her like buck-shot
when she's within four feet of his shirt,
shuns the dirt under his fingernails.

Thirty five years of living, her lifeline
drawn in therapy, jagged up and down, marks
all or nothing. It has become like him
printing her name, the date, with a stick.
Where he is sober. No. He is drunk. Sober
again, drunk.
there is no peace on her paper.
She knows it is his laziness
she envies most. Standing in yellow maple leaves
spread on cement, she wishes
for jasmine scented hot tubs, slow margaritas.
The ability to linger.

In October she walked up to him,
put her arms around his chest.
It was like free falling into a pile of leaves
for the first time.
Feeling his bony fingers dig into her skin
he steadied himself, grabbing her like his walker.

The sorrow in his eyes resembles mist
squeezed from the sky, and she held him close.
Pressing his whiskers into her chin,
dot impressions on her face, like buck shot's
scattered pattern. To pluck a goose.
How they have try to fly, and have to be clubbed

with the butt of the shotgun. Don't shoot grounded
geese,
ruins the meat. She pulled him in tighter,
like a shell in a chamber and held him
until she remembered nothing.

INTO MEDICINE BOW

Two strangers hiked a narrow trail
intent on reaching the peak.
They did not speak. He reached
the summit before her,
he stood like a carin.

Carrying their weighted differences,
together they gazed down upon ground
they would covet for the weekend.
They were heading to find camp spots
when something pulled them to stop.

And for a moment,
when the thin air, in its blueness
entered their lungs, bleaching their hearts,
long before their eyes met
past Medicine Bow, beyond speech,
drawn to touch the arm of a stranger
seized by alto cirrus in worship,
northward to the Snowy Range

where mountainous heaps of white heaved
its granite peaks toward the feet of God,
when for one-tenth of a second
before their feet lifted and levitated from rock
they stumbled and dropped through the skin of their
souls.

,

SHE WAITS

A promise of passage
is liken to loss. The insidious way
the sun's arc slips into
the northern hemisphere,
melting ice from antlers
discarded on the forest floor.

This need seems so clear
walking the woods.
Walking this meadow
overgrown with thick juniper,
a thicket of memories scrapping her skin.

Her back is truly strapped
with a frame pack,
suitable for survival.
It's belt frayed from weighted attachments,
canteen, compass. These hold
her back erect, straight like a pole pine.
A Buck knife hangs nudging her thigh.
It's horn handle notching losses,
fits her fist too well.

There is no way for her to relax
carrying tomorrow's water,
and she waits for the pictures in her mind
to be erased, and she waits
for a place of refuge and grace.

TWELVE MILES IN

Out my front door lay Spencer Street and cornfields,
black snakes and abandoned sheds.
A pasture from heaven,
or seems so now
where Danny and I'd race through rows
to the levee, head for Cache Creek
and catch crawdads in coffee cans.

We'd aim rocks at water, taking down
curled brown hickory leaves floating downstream
before they'd reach the marshy bend,
the end of the eddy,
of cattail stands and gumbo.

We were like colts
crossing a field,
one boy, one girl
running in wet grassland,
a span of fresh horses
extending the distance.

Today, twelve miles in,
years from him
and the Mississippi Valley,
backpacking in the Wind
River Mountains, he came to me
as an earthen smell, a damp cloud
hung like river fog, concealing

the passage where land and water blent.

I knelt in mud, I could not resist.
Raising one hand to my mouth and nose
I drew him in, again and again.
I like broken ground and he the mist,
I gazed skyward
toward a glacier heaving up
from moraine that touched
and engulfed the pasture
I played in as a kid.

TRINITY

It happened on a Thursday,
ordinary workday nine to five,
after my oldest daughter phoned
three times, once to read
our mail, a Sears bill,
balance thirty five. Again
complaining boredom, then to
whine of her younger sister's attitude.

It happened long after my shoes fell
to the blue linoleum and water
was cupped and splashed on my face,
droplets finding their way
to nest in my naval.
Long past the cricket found
housed and singing in our lilac.

It came about while we three sat
huddled on the stoop:
the slipping sun
exposed the evening sky
exultant in its emptiness,
but for the moon -
dripping full, like a mother's breast
spilling milk gently over our desert.

And there
to the right side of the moon

appeared a triangle, where three
perfect pools of cream
hung close to the earth and spun,
Juniper, Venus, Mars...
did we forget the June heat,
humdrum, and rocked
within earshot of heaven.

UP NORTH

Last night we watched the moon,
fish surfaced and bugs hit the lantern.
On an air mattress he sobbed,
asked me questions, said answer
as a woman, not a friend.
Ask how to face his x-wife
with her new boyfriend Earl.
Confided how he cries in the shower.
I saw his ribs rise slow, then he fell
into water.

Today in Jackson we go
for supplies, and he sees some girl with wet bangs.
How she shakes her messy hair in place,
one graceful movement of her neck,
her moves are smooth, confident
like the bass that flew
last night from the water's face
and took down mosquito hawks,
and how she stands
in line, like a doe on the edge of the lake
sucking down moonshine,
staggering back head raised, dripping
in the evening haze. He feels his cock
stirs in his jeans, and says to me, let's eat
at that sidewalk cafe.

Back in the truck leaving town

I could hear him yell
over the sound of gravel firing up from the ground
when he cried, God I am alive
and free. Pleading with me
to go back. Said drive
around the block again, said slow down,
said stop, as he leaned out the truck window
for another look.

CAMP NEAR FORT LACLEDE

Twenty one miles south of I-80
Bitter Creek and broken asphalt
race even and flat,
while chunks of gravel
scream up from, the earth
like small rockets, dinging my truck.

The range sleeps in November.
Desert air doesn't nap. It pierces
me with an invisible circle
of light, energy let loose unlike anything
I've ever know.

Even the woods and fields
back home, that age seven
spoke to me, even then holding oak leaves,
tickets to the world, my lyceum.
Even those things do not match it.
Here I search like a kid on a mission,
like I've never walked on this earth before.

The desert flats lay open and bare, free
of color, open like a mother's arm waiting
for the return of her children.
I look at the sky,
into accepting eyes

and I turn in all directions, I shout hallooo,
flinging my arms around
where I inhale the smell of glory,
passing through what soon will be snowfields.

WASHED AWAY

I went astray dad. My path muddied up.
I know I've disappointed you too many times.
Your love, and Christlike behaviors
have been drained and your stomach upset.

You lay not moving on the bed,
words have left you. My emotions hang heavy
like a river rock necklace, pulling my head down low.
I fear my self centered mess has shrunk your heart,
your love dried up, sending me on down the road.

I thought you would always be here, strong
like this house you built 65 years ago. This very
house
I grew up in. I thought I could always come back
home
to beg forgiveness.
But there were too many..

mistakes, marriages,
excuses, men, miles.
Too many times I didn't come back here.
Too many years..

I thought you knew you were my knight, and I need
you
proud of me, to know I love you with all my might.

But you wouldn't have known how much you were
loved.
No one would know, without being shown. Because
even
steadfast love can be washed away.

I've prayed for this chance to say I'm sorry.
I've fallen to my knees a thousand times.
I'm weighted down with heartache, regret..
please dad, please, forgive me.
I carry shame like a bouquet.

POURING RAIN

It never rains in Wyoming.
People get scared if it rains.
Stay off the road
should it sprinkle. If it ever rained
all day like it could along the Mississippi
they'd close the schools. The sage
would overtake the interstate.
They prefer snow here or dust.
4 wheel drives and chains.
Go to the mall in a blizzard,
pick sand out of their teeth.
I miss the smell of rain. The sound
it makes hitting the tin roof back home,
thunder rolling through the woods. Where a flash
means count... one hundred one
one hundred two...
Perhaps, that's why I choose to camp
by a creek. Or leave a window open
year round. And the colors
after rain passes, a fluorescent lamp
on the lawn.
Oh, I don't blame the people here
for the lack of rain. I guess
it's their fixed jeans and boots
attitude about it. Their inability to miss it.
When gardening in my yard
I feel raindrops tap my head,
water hits my skin and I have to grin

when I see my neighbor
open her curtains, then shut them quick,
when she sees me running
with my mouth open,
begging for more.

FINITE STATION

I have learned to honor the desert.
When bringing topo's and my pack
into Indian summer sage
I chalk pictures of lizards
sunning on lichen speckled rocks.

I think of the time
I first walked here
numb tongued, not even water
from my canteen eased my throat. Afraid
to leave the truck, looking into flats
that hid rattlesnakes under ledges,
fossilized fish. Abandoned
drilling pads and Overland Trail ruts
waiting to be reclaimed.

This land is dangerously lean.
A steppe, like a Precambrian shelf,
could change me, as freely
as I could disappear from rim to rim...
having nothing to hold but sand.
As simply as
bones return to the range,
taken back to be cleaned.
I've seen the evidence
jutting out of dirt,
a green stoned femur.
It seemed so logical then.

But today, I come addicted,
my feet crave the edge
of origin or end,
and now I think I'll hike
south to the Gates Of Lodore,
toward a squall line
sweeping the distant ridge,
strip
and tap dance
on the desert floor.